BMW

CLASSIC MOTORCYCLES

BMW

HUGO WILSON

DORLING KINDERSLEY
LONDON • NEW YORK • SYDNEY • MOSCOW

A DORLING KINDERSLEY BOOK

DESIGNED & EDITED BY
Mark Johnson Davies & Phil Hunt

SENIOR EDITOR
Louise Candlish

SENIOR ART EDITOR
Heather McCarry

MANAGING EDITOR
Anna Kruger

DEPUTY ART DIRECTOR
Tina Vaughan

PRODUCTION CONTROLLER
Alison Jones

First published in Great Britain in 1998 by Dorling Kindersley Limited
9 Henrietta Street, London WC2E 8PS

2 4 6 8 10 9 7 5 3 1

A CIP catalogue record for this book is available from the British Library

ISBN 0 7513 0627 4

Reproduced by Colourscan, Singapore
Printed in Hong Kong

CONTENTS

INTRODUCTION
10-11

BMW TIMELINE
12-13

1923 R32
14-15

1928 R63
16-17

1931 R2
18-19

1935 R12
20-21

1939 KOMPRESSOR
22-23

1954 RENNSPORT
24-25

1958 R26
26-27

1961 R69/S
28-29

1965 R60
30-31

1971 R75/5
32-33

1975 R90/S
34-35

1992 K1
36-37

1994 R1100GS
38-39

1997 F650ST
40-41

1997 R1100RT
42-43

INDEX &
ACKNOWLEDGEMENTS
44

INTRODUCTION

Circumstances forced BMW to diversify
into motorcycle manufacture at the end
of World War I. The company applied
to its motorcycles the principles of
ingenuity, quality, and practicality that
had previously served it in the
aeronautical business, and soon
achieved an enviable reputation for
the quality and cost of its machines.
Seventy-five years after the first BMW
was designed, that reputation is still in
place. Such was the farsightedness
of the original design, the 1100cc
fuel-injected BMW of today is a direct
descendent of that first machine.

HUGO WILSON

BMW TIMELINE

BMW HAS A TRADITION OF technical innovation combined with a long-standing devotion to the flat-twin engine and shaft drive layout which it has been using since it began motorcycle production in 1923. The company's desire to produce reliable, useable motorcycles means that while it is committed to innovation and quality of construction, it has never indulged in change for its own sake.

R32

THE EARLY DAYS

The R32 used a tubular frame construction with period trailing-link front forks. It was more integrated than most contemporary machines, but still needed a sprung saddle as there was no rear suspension.

• 1910s	• 1920s	• 1930s	• 1940s	•

THE 1950s

BMW reverted to tubular frames for some bikes in 1936, and two years later adopted a crude rear suspension system. In 1955, it revised its bike design to include swingarm suspension on the rear and on the front fork.

R12

THE 1930s

The R12 used a pressed-steel frame, which BMW had first offered on its singles in 1929. The bike's innovation was in its hydraulically damped telescopic front fork, four-speed gearbox, and rear drum brake.

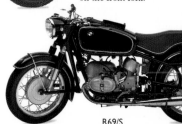

R69/S

BREAKING WITH TRADITION

In the 1980s, BMW thought it had to move away from the twin-cylinder engine to compete with other manufacturers. Its range of three- and four-cylinder superbikes, of which this 1992 K1 is an example, was launched in 1983. However, the company soon reverted to the flat twin.

BMW retained shaft drive on the K1

K1

• 1960s	• 1970s	• 1980s	• 1990s

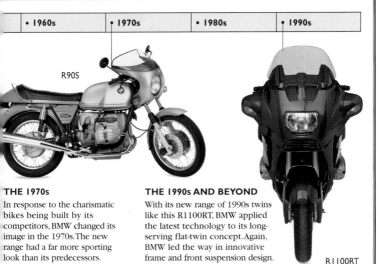

R90S

R1100RT

THE 1970s

In response to the charismatic bikes being built by its competitors, BMW changed its image in the 1970s. The new range had a far more sporting look than its predecessors.

THE 1990s AND BEYOND

With its new range of 1990s twins like this R1100RT, BMW applied the latest technology to its long-serving flat-twin concept. Again, BMW led the way in innovative frame and front suspension design.

1923 R32

• A GROUND-BREAKING BIKE FROM BMW •

At a time when most motorcycles were still crude and impractical
devices, the R32 was a revelation. Introduced at the 1923 Paris Show,
it had a unitary engine/gearbox assembly and shaft final drive. The
automatic lubrication system used oil stored in the engine's sump, and
the combination of this system, shaft drive, and valanced mudguards
made it an exceptionally clean and practical machine. The gearbox had
three speeds and was mounted with the engine in a tubular cradle
frame fitted with trailing-link leaf-sprung front suspension. The quality
of construction made the BMW considerably more expensive than its
competitors, but the originality of the design guaranteed its success.

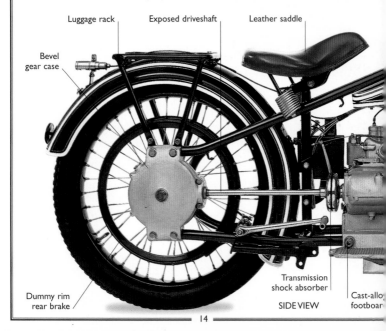

Luggage rack   Exposed driveshaft   Leather saddle

Bevel
gear case

Transmission
shock absorber

Cast-alloy
footboar

SIDE VIEW

Dummy rim
rear brake

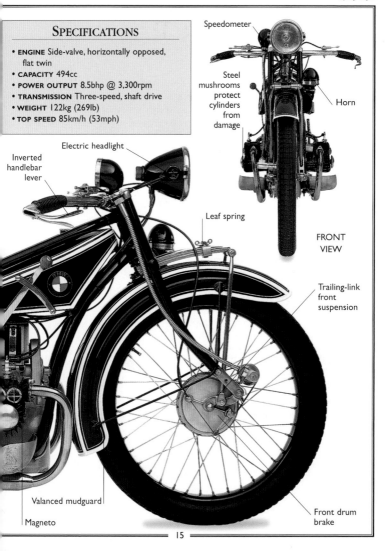

SPECIFICATIONS

- **ENGINE** Side-valve, horizontally opposed, flat twin
- **CAPACITY** 494cc
- **POWER OUTPUT** 8.5bhp @ 3,300rpm
- **TRANSMISSION** Three-speed, shaft drive
- **WEIGHT** 122kg (269lb)
- **TOP SPEED** 85km/h (53mph)

Speedometer

Steel mushrooms protect cylinders from damage

Horn

FRONT VIEW

Electric headlight

Inverted handlebar lever

Leaf spring

Trailing-link front suspension

Valanced mudguard

Magneto

Front drum brake

1928 R63

• A MORE ROBUST VERSION OF THE R32 •

BMW SOON INCREASED THE POWER of its original 500cc side-valve twin by fitting overhead valvegear. In 1928, power was increased again by raising the engine capacity to 750cc and the new machine was dubbed the R63. Unlike most contemporary overhead-valve machines, the valvegear was completely enclosed, resulting in a cleaner and quieter engine. The brakes were also uprated, with a transmission brake replacing the dummy rim on the R32 and a larger front drum fitted.

Fuel tank has knee pads

Large-diameter drum brake

Alloy rocker covers hide valvegear

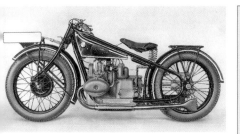

SPECIFICATIONS

- **ENGINE** Overhead-valve, horizontally opposed twin
- **CAPACITY** 734cc
- **POWER OUTPUT** 24bhp @ 4,000rpm
- **TRANSMISSION** Three-speed, shaft drive
- **WEIGHT** 155kg (342lb)
- **TOP SPEED** 120km/h (75mph)

QUALITY AT A PRICE

While the R63 was one of the most impressive and well-made bikes available to motorcyclists in the 1920s, it came at a price. In 1931, the model was listed in the UK at £128, while a BSA of similar capacity was available for £58.

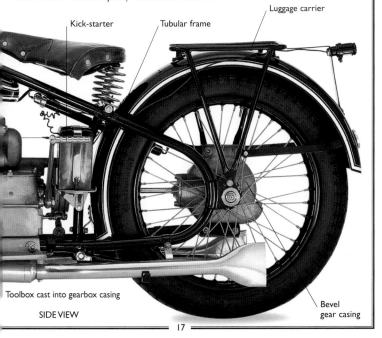

Luggage carrier

Kick-starter   Tubular frame

Toolbox cast into gearbox casing

SIDE VIEW

Bevel gear casing

1931 R2
• AN ECONOMICAL MACHINE FOR A THRIFTY ERA •

GERMANY FELT THE MOST SEVERE effects of the worldwide recession of the late 1920s and, with manufacturing industry particularly badly hit, cost became the major consideration in motorcycle production. BMW responded by introducing a utilitarian *Volksmotorrad* (people's motorcycle), the R2, in 1931. This model was effectively half a twin, with the cylinder mounted vertically and the 198cc engine capacity chosen to comply with German tax regulations. To make efficient use of the bike's small capacity, the engine was offset to the right of the frame, allowing a straight drive line in top gear. Despite cost-cutting measures such as exposed valvegear and minimal use of electroplating, the price of the R2 was actually twice that of some competitors.

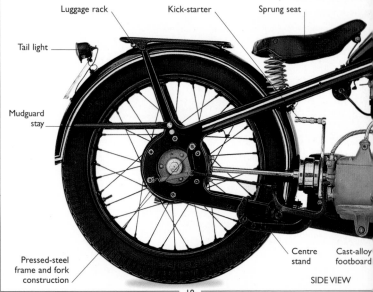

Luggage rack

Kick-starter

Sprung seat

Tail light

Mudguard stay

Pressed-steel frame and fork construction

Centre stand

Cast-alloy footboard

SIDE VIEW

SPECIFICATIONS

- **ENGINE** Overhead-valve, single cylinder
- **CAPACITY** 198cc
- **POWER OUTPUT** 6bhp @ 3,500rpm
- **TRANSMISSION** Three-speed, shaft drive
- **WEIGHT** 110kg (242lb)
- **TOP SPEED** 95km/h (59mph)

A NEW MARKET FOR BMW

The R2 was built to take advantage of new German tax laws, which offered concessions to bikes under 200cc. These small-capacity bikes suddenly became attractive to people seeking mobility.

Exposed valvegear

Leaf-spring front suspension

Pressed-steel fork

Gears selected by handchange lever

Mudguard stay is also front stand

1935 R12

• TECHNOLOGICAL ADVANCES PUSH THE R12 TO THE FORE •

BMW MAINTAINED ITS TECHNOLOGICAL lead over other manufacturers with the introduction, in 1935, of the R12 and its overhead-valve sister, the R17. These were the first production bikes to use the hydraulically damped telescopic forks that are still a feature of motorcycle design today. The R12 had a pressed-steel frame construction, which was used by several manufacturers at that time, and a four-speed gearbox.

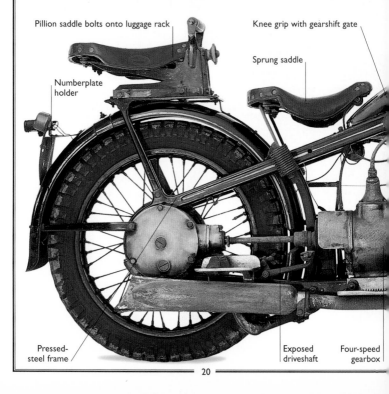

Pillion saddle bolts onto luggage rack

Knee grip with gearshift gate

Sprung saddle

Numberplate holder

Pressed-steel frame

Exposed driveshaft

Four-speed gearbox

SPECIFICATIONS

- **ENGINE** Side-valve, horizontally opposed twin
- **CAPACITY** 745cc
- **POWER OUTPUT** 20bhp @ 4,000rpm
- **TRANSMISSION** Four-speed, shaft drive
- **WEIGHT** 188kg (414lb)
- **TOP SPEED** 120km/h (75mph)

MASS PRODUCTION

The R12 was produced in vast
numbers at BMW's factory in Munich.
It retained some styling features from
BMW's first bike, made back in 1923.

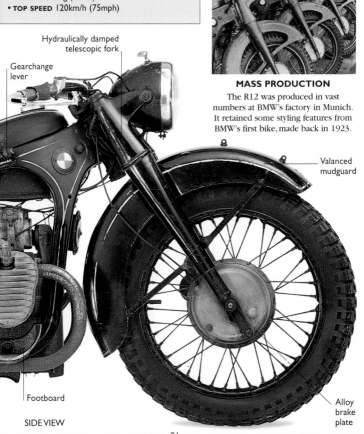

Hydraulically damped
telescopic fork

Gearchange
lever

Valanced
mudguard

Footboard

SIDE VIEW

Alloy
brake
plate

1939 KOMPRESSOR

• THE PRE-WAR RACING SENSATION •

BEFORE WORLD WAR II, German motorcycle manufacturers were
encouraged by the government to compete in international races.
In 1935, BMW, who had previously concentrated on off-road competition
and speed-record attempts, produced this new 500cc road racer, which
featured overhead camshafts and a supercharger. The power output was
about twice that of the British-built singles that had previously been
the benchmark bikes. Herman Meier won the European Championship
on a Kompressor in 1938 and the Senior TT the following year.

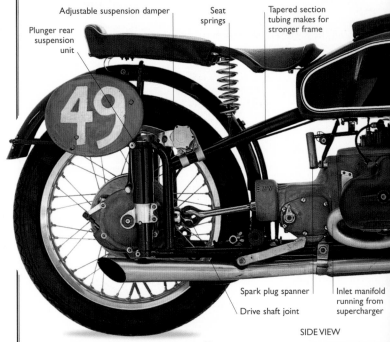

Adjustable suspension damper

Seat
springs

Tapered section
tubing makes for
stronger frame

Plunger rear
suspension
unit

Spark plug spanner

Inlet manifold
running from
supercharger

Drive shaft joint

SIDE VIEW

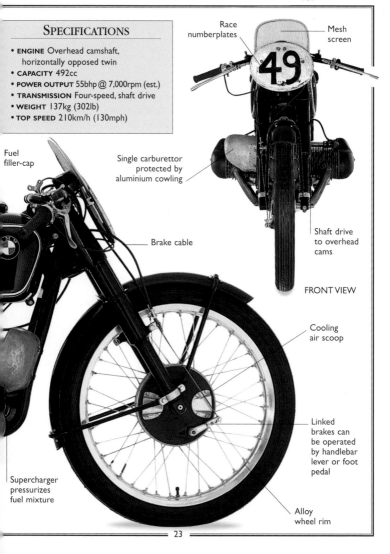

SPECIFICATIONS

- **ENGINE** Overhead camshaft, horizontally opposed twin
- **CAPACITY** 492cc
- **POWER OUTPUT** 55bhp @ 7,000rpm (est.)
- **TRANSMISSION** Four-speed, shaft drive
- **WEIGHT** 137kg (302lb)
- **TOP SPEED** 210km/h (130mph)

Race numberplates

Mesh screen

Fuel filler-cap

Single carburettor protected by aluminium cowling

Brake cable

Shaft drive to overhead cams

FRONT VIEW

Cooling air scoop

Linked brakes can be operated by handlebar lever or foot pedal

Supercharger pressurizes fuel mixture

Alloy wheel rim

1954 RENNSPORT
• BMW'S POST-SUPERCHARGING CHARGER •

SUPERCHARGING WAS BANNED BY THE **FIM** (Federation of International Motorcyclists) after World War II and BMW responded by introducing a new racing machine in 1954. While retaining the traditional BMW layout, the Rennsport was an all-new bike. It had a tubular cradle frame with swingarm rear suspension and each cylinder had an overhead cam driven by shaft and bevel gears. Both carburettors and fuel injection versions were produced. While the bike never won a solo Grand Prix, in sidecar racing it proved almost invincible, winning 18 World Championships.

Earles forks were stronger than telescopics and ideal for sidecar events

Magneto is gear driven from front of engine

Twin leading-shoe drum brake

Dell'Orto carburettors

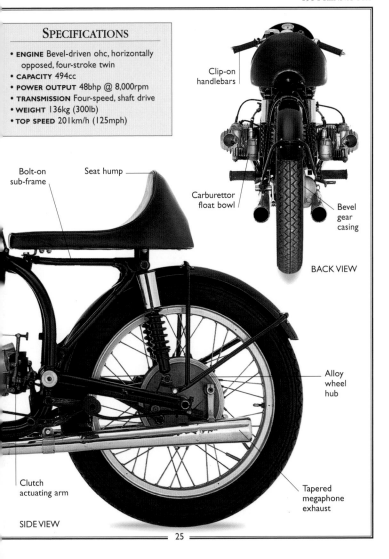

SPECIFICATIONS

- **ENGINE** Bevel-driven ohc, horizontally opposed, four-stroke twin
- **CAPACITY** 494cc
- **POWER OUTPUT** 48bhp @ 8,000rpm
- **TRANSMISSION** Four-speed, shaft drive
- **WEIGHT** 136kg (300lb)
- **TOP SPEED** 201km/h (125mph)

Clip-on handlebars

Carburettor float bowl

Bevel gear casing

BACK VIEW

Bolt-on sub-frame

Seat hump

Alloy wheel hub

Clutch actuating arm

Tapered megaphone exhaust

SIDE VIEW

1958 R26

• A LUXURY 250 WITH THE ACCENT ON COMFORT •

BMW CONTINUED TO OFFER ITS half-a-twin singles after World War II. These shared many features with the two-cylinder bikes and so were well made, comfortable, and reliable. Unfortunately, it also meant that they weighed almost as much as the larger models while producing half the power. What's more, their performance was worse, and their cost far greater, than most other 250s. By the mid-1960s, buyers looking for a good-quality four-stroke 250 could buy a Honda and have change to spare. Most of them did, and BMW discontinued its singles in 1967. It was another quarter of a century before BMW produced another single, but the new bike had no similarities with the company's twins.

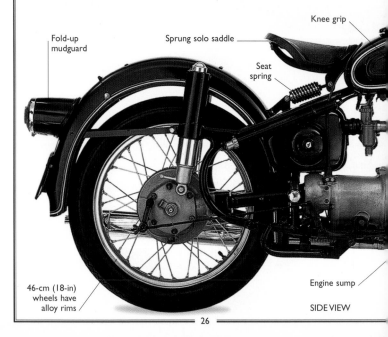

Knee grip

Fold-up mudguard

Sprung solo saddle

Seat spring

46-cm (18-in) wheels have alloy rims

Engine sump

SIDE VIEW

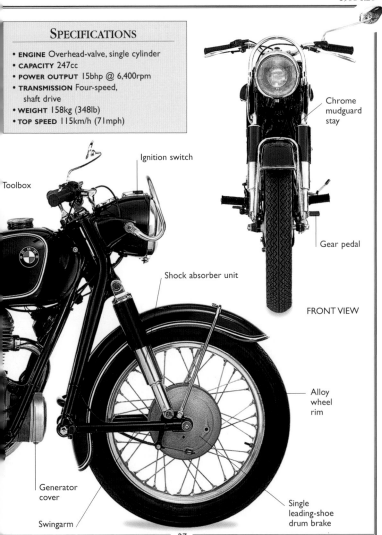

SPECIFICATIONS

- **ENGINE** Overhead-valve, single cylinder
- **CAPACITY** 247cc
- **POWER OUTPUT** 15bhp @ 6,400rpm
- **TRANSMISSION** Four-speed, shaft drive
- **WEIGHT** 158kg (348lb)
- **TOP SPEED** 115km/h (71mph)

Chrome mudguard stay

Ignition switch

Toolbox

Gear pedal

Shock absorber unit

FRONT VIEW

Alloy wheel rim

Generator cover

Swingarm

Single leading-shoe drum brake

1961 R69/S

• THE BEST BMW EVER PRODUCED? •

THE R69/S WAS A SPORTING VERSION of BMW's rather staid 600cc twin and was produced between 1959 and 1969. The power output was boosted by increasing the compression ratio to 9.5:1 and a close ratio gearbox was fitted. Cycle parts were similar to the standard R60 model. For high-speed touring the R69/S was the benchmark motorcycle in the late 1950s and early 1960s, and for some enthusiasts it represents the best BMW ever built. This 1961 example is fitted with an after-market large-capacity fuel tank.

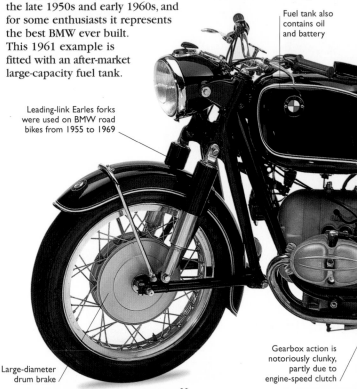

Fuel tank also contains oil and battery

Leading-link Earles forks were used on BMW road bikes from 1955 to 1969

Large-diameter drum brake

Gearbox action is notoriously clunky, partly due to engine-speed clutch

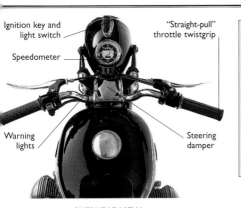

Ignition key and
light switch

Speedometer

"Straight-pull"
throttle twistgrip

Warning
lights

Steering
damper

OVERHEAD VIEW

SPECIFICATIONS

- **ENGINE** Overhead-valve,
  horizontally opposed
  twin
- **CAPACITY** 594cc
- **POWER OUTPUT** 42bhp
- **TRANSMISSION**
  Four-speed, shaft
  drive
- **WEIGHT** 202kg (445lb)
- **TOP SPEED** 177km/h
  (110mph)

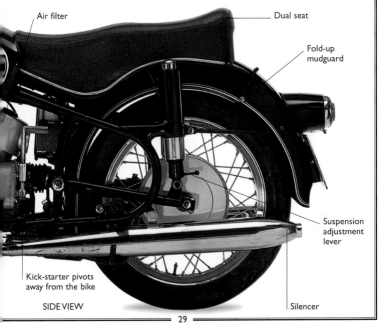

Air filter

Dual seat

Fold-up
mudguard

Suspension
adjustment
lever

Kick-starter pivots
away from the bike

SIDE VIEW

Silencer

1965 R60
• THE POPULAR CHOICE FOR A SIDECAR •

HAVING BEGUN POST-WAR PRODUCTION with pre-war models, BMW's road bikes were comprehensively redesigned in 1955. The front and rear suspension on the new frames was provided by pivoting forks. The steering geometry and the strength of the new front suspension was ideal for sidecar use, and the BMW became the definitive sidecar machine. The combination shown here consists of a 1965 R60 mated to the classic German-built Steib sidecar. Special sidecar gearing was offered by most manufacturers, which helped the bikes pull the extra weight of the "chair", though performance was obviously reduced. Steib sidecars were built at Nürnberg from the late 1920s and were noted for their quality. While the arrival of cheap motorcars in the 1950s ended the widespread popularity of sidecars, they retain a hard core of committed enthusiasts.

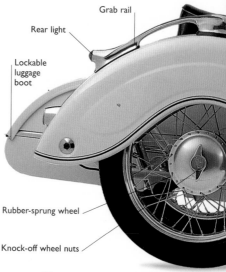

Grab rail

Rear light

Lockable luggage boot

Rubber-sprung wheel

Knock-off wheel nuts

STEIB CATALOGUE
BMW and Zündapp buyers could order their new bike with a Steib attached. Steib offered a variety of models for both motorcycle and scooter owners.

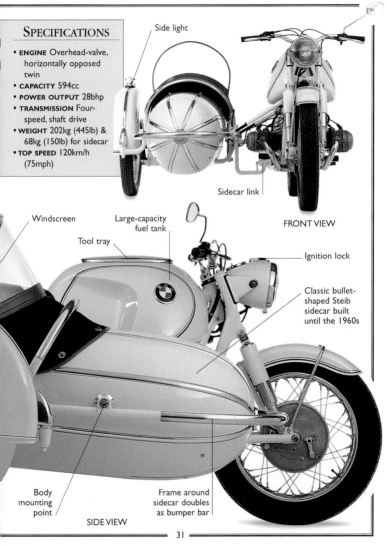

SPECIFICATIONS

- **ENGINE** Overhead-valve, horizontally opposed twin
- **CAPACITY** 594cc
- **POWER OUTPUT** 28bhp
- **TRANSMISSION** Four-speed, shaft drive
- **WEIGHT** 202kg (445lb) & 68kg (150lb) for sidecar
- **TOP SPEED** 120km/h (75mph)

Side light

Sidecar link

FRONT VIEW

Windscreen

Large-capacity fuel tank

Tool tray

Ignition lock

Classic bullet-shaped Steib sidecar built until the 1960s

Body mounting point

Frame around sidecar doubles as bumper bar

SIDE VIEW

1971 R75/5
• RUGGED SIMPLICITY WITH A CHOICE OF ENGINE SIZES •

In 1969, BMW INTRODUCED A NEW RANGE of twins to replace its ageing line-up. The new /5 Series was available in 500, 600, and 750cc capacities. The engines were all-new, with the camshaft now mounted below the crank and the telescopic front fork returning to replace the leading-link design used on previous models. Die-hard fans bemoaned a (slight) drop in quality, but the /5 Series continued BMW's tradition of reliability, easy maintenance, and comfort, while offering increased performance. A range of accessories, from large-capacity fuel tanks to hard panniers, was available to improve further the bikes' touring capability.

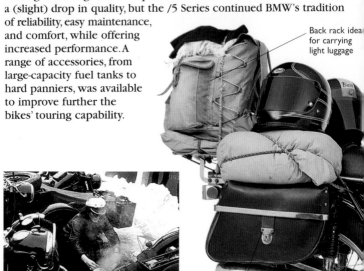

Back rack ideal for carrying light luggage

Panniers fitted to either side of rear wheel

MOTORCYCLE TOURING
While "credit card tourers" require no more than a change of clothing and a well-stocked wallet, others, like those above, feel the need to take everything but the kitchen sink.

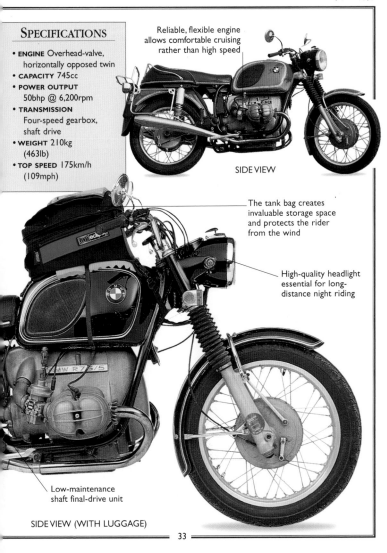

SPECIFICATIONS

- **ENGINE** Overhead-valve, horizontally opposed twin
- **CAPACITY** 745cc
- **POWER OUTPUT** 50bhp @ 6,200rpm
- **TRANSMISSION** Four-speed gearbox, shaft drive
- **WEIGHT** 210kg (463lb)
- **TOP SPEED** 175km/h (109mph)

Reliable, flexible engine allows comfortable cruising rather than high speed

SIDE VIEW

The tank bag creates invaluable storage space and protects the rider from the wind

High-quality headlight essential for long-distance night riding

Low-maintenance shaft final-drive unit

SIDE VIEW (WITH LUGGAGE)

1975 R90/S

• BMW UNLEASHES A FAST AND FASHIONABLE NEW MACHINE •

HAVING SUCCESFULLY REVISED ITS MACHINES with the introduction of the /5 Series in 1969, BMW sought to improve the bikes further and change their conservative image with the /6 series, launched in 1973. Flagship of the new range was the 900cc R90/S. This was the fastest and most powerful road bike the company had ever built and, when finished in the smoke orange paint scheme shown here, the most colourful. Its increased power and performance helped to convince doubters that BMW could produce exciting machines. BMW fitted hydraulic disc brakes for the first time on these bikes.

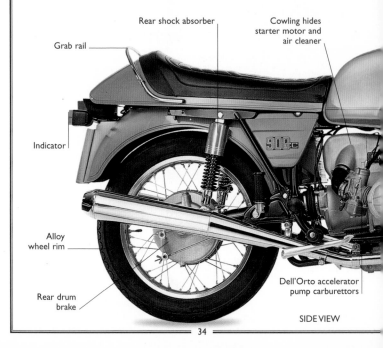

Rear shock absorber

Cowling hides
starter motor and
air cleaner

Grab rail

Indicator

Alloy
wheel rim

Rear drum
brake

Dell'Orto accelerator
pump carburettors

SIDE VIEW

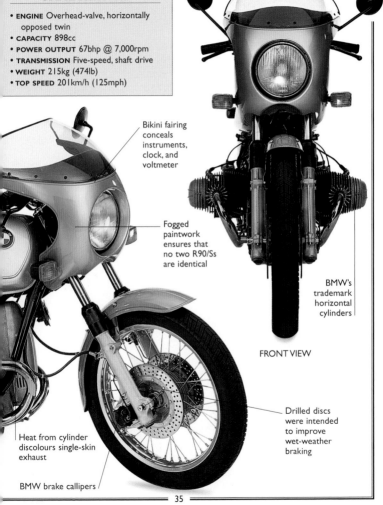

SPECIFICATIONS

- **ENGINE** Overhead-valve, horizontally opposed twin
- **CAPACITY** 898cc
- **POWER OUTPUT** 67bhp @ 7,000rpm
- **TRANSMISSION** Five-speed, shaft drive
- **WEIGHT** 215kg (474lb)
- **TOP SPEED** 201km/h (125mph)

Bikini fairing conceals instruments, clock, and voltmeter

Fogged paintwork ensures that no two R90/Ss are identical

BMW's trademark horizontal cylinders

FRONT VIEW

Heat from cylinder discolours single-skin exhaust

BMW brake callipers

Drilled discs were intended to improve wet-weather braking

1992 K1

• A FLAGSHIP BIKE WITH IMPRESSIVE FEATURES •

Sᴛʀɪᴄᴛ ɴᴇᴡ ɴᴏɪsᴇ ʀᴇsᴛʀɪᴄᴛɪᴏɴs ᴛʜʀᴇᴀᴛᴇɴᴇᴅ BMW's old-fashioned air-cooled twins with extinction in the 1980s. The company responded by introducing from 1983 a range of three- and four-cylinder fuel-injected and water-cooled machines that retained the shaft drive and used a unique engine layout. The radical-looking K1 was introduced in 1990. Under the aerodynamic skin it had anti-lock brakes, paralever rear suspension, and a revised engine with four valves per cylinder.

Low screen

Unique BMW switchgear

Aerodynamic fairing designed in wind tunnel

Air duct

Three-spoke alloy wheel

Anti-lock braking trigger

Radiator air vent

SIDE VIEW

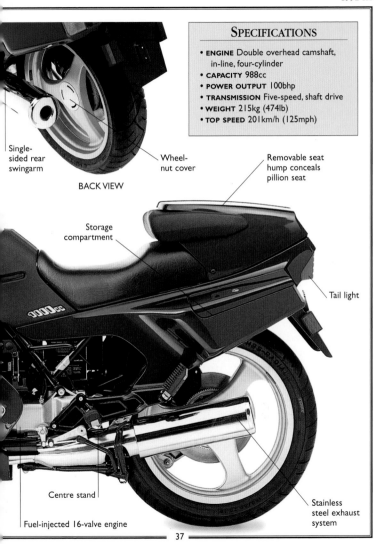

SPECIFICATIONS

- **ENGINE** Double overhead camshaft, in-line, four-cylinder
- **CAPACITY** 988cc
- **POWER OUTPUT** 100bhp
- **TRANSMISSION** Five-speed, shaft drive
- **WEIGHT** 215kg (474lb)
- **TOP SPEED** 201km/h (125mph)

Single-sided rear swingarm

Wheel-nut cover

BACK VIEW

Removable seat hump conceals pillion seat

Storage compartment

Tail light

Centre stand

Stainless steel exhaust system

Fuel-injected 16-valve engine

1994 R1100GS

• INNOVATIVE DESIGN ON A TRADITIONAL BLOCK •

SEVENTY YEARS AFTER ITS FIRST SHAFT DRIVE flat-twin, BMW introduced
a new range of radical machines based on that original layout. The
new engines had eight valves and fuel injection, but the real
innovation was in the chassis. Front suspension was by a new
"Telelever" system that dispensed with a telescopic fork and
much of the frame, now only made up of two minimalist sub-
frames on which the steering head and the seat were mounted.
Several models with 850 and 1100cc engines were available.

Alloy grab rail

Bosch fuel injection

Footrest

Adjustable
seat height

Short
exhaust

Shaft final drive

Engine protector

Torque arm

Front suspension wishbone

SPECIFICATIONS

- **ENGINE** Eight-valve, horizontally opposed twin
- **CAPACITY** 1085CC
- **POWER OUTPUT** 80bhp @ 6,750rpm
- **TRANSMISSION** Five-speed, shaft drive
- **WEIGHT** 209kg (460lb)
- **TOP SPEED** 214km/h (133mph)

Front suspension wishbone

Rear shock absorber

MINIMAL FRAME (FROM R1100RS)

Windscreen

Instrument and mudguard mounting

Four-valve cylinder head

Offset spokes allow use of tubeless tyres

48-cm (19-in) front wheel with alloy rim

Front fork

SIDE VIEW

FRONT VIEW

1997 F650ST

• BMW BREAKS THE MOULD •

The F650 is a truly European motorcycle. Conceived by BMW in Germany, it is assembled by Aprilia in Italy using a single-cylinder engine built in Austria by Rotax. This is a remarkable machine for BMW; it is the first single-cylinder BMW for 25 years and the first ever to feature chain drive. The F650 was launched in 1993 with the intention of attracting new buyers to the marque, and its light, practical, fun composition makes it an ideal bike for inexperienced riders.

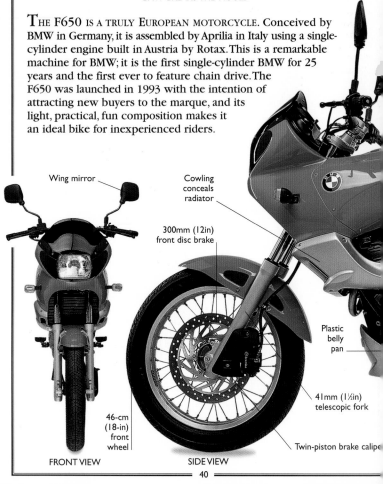

Wing mirror

Cowling conceals radiator

300mm (12in) front disc brake

Plastic belly pan

46-cm (18-in) front wheel

41mm (1½in) telescopic fork

Twin-piston brake caliper

FRONT VIEW

SIDE VIEW

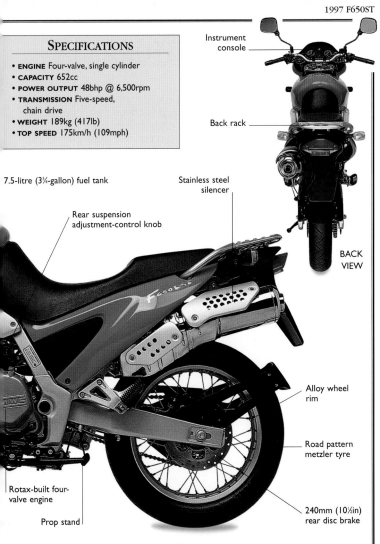

SPECIFICATIONS

- **ENGINE** Four-valve, single cylinder
- **CAPACITY** 652cc
- **POWER OUTPUT** 48bhp @ 6,500rpm
- **TRANSMISSION** Five-speed,
  chain drive
- **WEIGHT** 189kg (417lb)
- **TOP SPEED** 175km/h (109mph)

Instrument console

Back rack

BACK VIEW

7.5-litre (3¾-gallon) fuel tank

Stainless steel silencer

Rear suspension adjustment-control knob

Alloy wheel rim

Road pattern metzler tyre

Rotax-built four-valve engine

Prop stand

240mm (10½in) rear disc brake

1997 R1100RT

• THE TRANSCONTINENTAL LUXURY TOURER •

THIS FULLY EQUIPPED TOURING VERSION of BMW's range of eight-valve twins appeared in 1995 and reaffirmed BMW as the supreme manufacturer of high-mileage motorcycles. The RT has a massive, and highly effective, fairing and an adjustable seat, making everyday riding a pleasure. It has the same engine and chassis layout – featuring the innovative telelever front suspension – as the other twins in the BMW range, but is equipped with all the luggage-carrying and luxury features that are valuable on a touring machine.

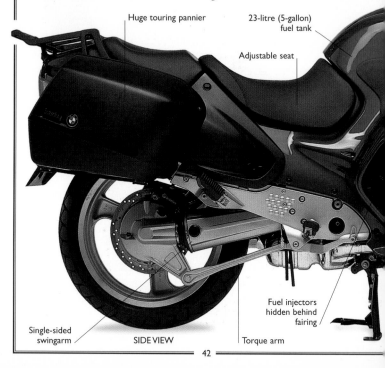

Huge touring pannier

23-litre (5-gallon)
fuel tank

Adjustable seat

Single-sided
swingarm

SIDE VIEW

Torque arm

Fuel injectors
hidden behind
fairing

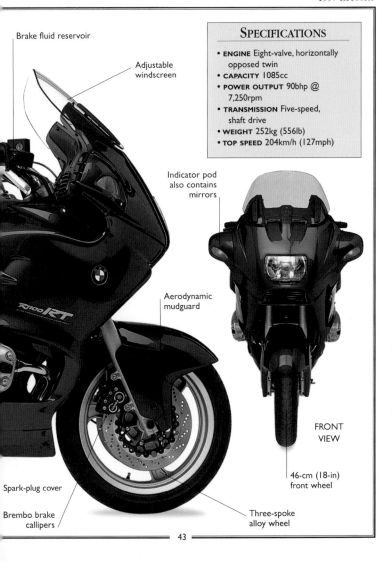

Brake fluid reservoir

Adjustable
windscreen

SPECIFICATIONS

- **ENGINE** Eight-valve, horizontally
  opposed twin
- **CAPACITY** 1085cc
- **POWER OUTPUT** 90bhp @
  7,250rpm
- **TRANSMISSION** Five-speed,
  shaft drive
- **WEIGHT** 252kg (556lb)
- **TOP SPEED** 204km/h (127mph)

Indicator pod
also contains
mirrors

Aerodynamic
mudguard

FRONT
VIEW

46-cm (18-in)
front wheel

Spark-plug cover

Brembo brake
callipers

Three-spoke
alloy wheel

INDEX

ABC

accessories 32
Aprilia 40
British singles 22
BSA 17
credit-card tourers 32

DE

Elephant Rally 32
European Championships 22

FGH

/5 Series 32, 34
/6 Series 34
F650 40-41
FIM (Federation
  of International
  Motorcyclists) 24
Grand Prix 24
high-speed touring 28
Honda 24

IJK

K1 13, 36-37
Kompressor 22-23

LMN

Meier, Hermann 22
noise restrictions 36
Nürnberg 30

OP

off-road competition 22
paralever suspension 36
Paris Show (1923) 40

QRST

R2 18-19
R12 12, 20-21
R17 20
R26 26-27

R32 11, 12, 14-15, 16
R60 28, 30-31
R63 16-17
R69/S 12, 28-29
R75/5 32-33
R90/S 13, 34-35
R1100GS 39-39
R1100RT 13, 42-43
recession, effects of 18
Rennsport 24-25
Rotax 40
speed-record attempts 22
Steib sidecars 30
supercharging 22, 24
Telelever system 38, 42
tubular cradle frame 24

UVWXYZ

World Championships 24
World War I 11
World War II 22, 24, 26
Zündapp 30

ACKNOWLEDGEMENTS

AUTHOR'S ACKNOWLEDGEMENTS:
Thanks to Phil Hunt and Mark Johnson-Davies
and to Louise Candlish, Tracy Hambleton-Miles,
and everyone else at DK. Thanks also to Emma
Goode, Paul Andrews, and David Taylor of
BMW (UK). Special thanks to Bertie, Dan, and
Jeff for their encyclopedic knowledge of BMW
part numbers.

**DORLING KINDERSLEY WOULD LIKE TO THANK
THE FOLLOWING FOR THEIR ASSISTANCE:**
BMW of America; Paul Davies, Park Lane Ltd.,
70 Park Lane, London; Deutsches Zweirad
Museum NSU Museum, Neckarsulm, Germany;
Emma Goode at BMW (GB) Ltd.; Russ Harris,
John Lawes, Motorcycle Heritage Foundation,
Westerville, Ohio, USA; The National Motor

Museum, Beaulieu; The National Motorcycle
Museum, Birmingham; and John Surtees.

**DORLING KINDERSLEY WOULD LIKE TO THANK
THE FOLLOWING FOR THEIR KIND PERMISSION
TO USE THEIR PHOTOGRAPHS:**

BMW AG: 17 top left, 19 top right, 21 top right,
32 bottom left, 33 top right.

All photography by Dave King and Andy Crawford.

NOTE
Every effort has been made to trace the copyright
holders. Dorling Kindersley apologizes for any
unintentional omissions and would be pleased,
in such cases, to add an acknowledgement in
future editions.